Who Am I? W]
Soul.

Table of Contents

Foreward
1. Cricklade 7 - 11
2. The Early Years 12 - 16
3. Lily-Rose 17 - 20
4. Séances 21 - 25
5. Psychic Tools 26 - 29
6. Sunderland 30 - 32
7. Monkwearmouth Grammar School 33 - 38
8. Canada 39 - 42
9. Maple Arbour Farm 43 - 52
10. The Onandaga United Church 53 - 57
11. Healing 58 - 60
12. Kitchener 61 - 66
13. Calgary 79 - 81
14. New Age Books, & Crystals 82 - 86
15. Ghosts, & speaking from the afterlife 87 - 88
16. Mediumship 89 - 91
17. Past Life Regressions 92 - 97
18. Evil 98 - 102
19. Miracles 1043 - 108
20. Our Souls 109 - 123
21. Soul Lessons Learned 124 - 125
22. Pictures 67 - 78

Foreward

I was born in Minchinhampton, a small hamlet in the UK. Minchinhampton is a delightful market town located 100 miles west of London. I was born at hillside farm just 2 miles from the town centre. I am the 3rd child of 4. I remember the farm quite clearly, even though we left when I was only four years old.

My father was a farmer, and my mother was a nurse. Memories from this time are the basis of my knowledge of the spirit world. The farm is a dairy farm with chickens, pigs, and sheep. It is super pretty there, the views are amazing. As the farm is nearly at the top of the hill, you can look out the windows of my bedroom and see for miles. The countryside is beautiful, the shades of green change across the pastures. You can see the sheep and cows grazing. The hills seem to roll by. One of my favorite things to do was to sit in the grass. Making daisy chains, as I look at the clouds in the sky.

When I was three years old or thereabouts, I woke up to a lot of noise, sirens blasting, and people talking. An ambulance had arrived to take my mother away. It was so frightening to see her taken away on a stretcher. I could see my father in a panic, and my mother was being given needles and was screaming with pain. I ran to my brothers, and we watched in terror as the men took her away from us. I had no idea what was happening; I don't think my brothers did either. My father was distraught and visibly shaking. He told David, my 8-year-old brother, to look after Grahame and I. Dad took Susan my little sister, who was only nine months old and drove off in the car. David took Grahame and me back into the house, where the three of us just sat and cried. We were so scared I asked David what happened and he just shook his head it was as if he couldn't speak.

It seemed like ages before dad returned with Susan and our neighbor. Dad said he brought Mrs. White to take care of us. Dad told us everything would be fine. He said he would be back soon with Mum. However, he was obviously very worried himself. I still remember the neighbor clearly. She was about the same age as my Mum, and I played with her son Philip a lot. I liked Mrs. White; she was so kind to us that night. She told us to pray for my Mum. Mrs. White said prayers get answered, and Mum would be home soon.

Then we all prayed together before she tucked us all back into our beds. Then as I lay trying to sleep, I felt as if I left my body. It was so eerie, I was floating and felt nothing. I could see all around me. I could see my mother lying on a bed with men in white coats standing around her. Tubes were hung to her arms, and my father was standing by the bed, I felt a whoosh, and I saw my Mum start to walk away from her body, and I followed her. Mum did not see or hear me, as I was calling her name. Mum never looked up or at me. I could tell I was invisible to her.

I can't say I was scared, but I know I felt so curious this was a very different feeling. I watched as my mum went into this tunnel that was filled with warmth and light. The tunnel was very dusty, and it looked very long. I followed my Mum as she started to walk, and I could hear her thoughts in my mind. Mum was so tired and had felt so cold that it felt nice to be in this warm tunnel. As mum looked ahead, I knew she could feel love all around her. I knew that because I thought it too. Mum was confused yet seemed so very calm. I looked back and could see my Father still sitting beside mum's body. Although I was with my Mum, I knew Mum was no longer with my father.

I could see my father crying. I was so upset and scared for him and our family. I asked myself what would happen if mum isn't with us? My Mum was still walking in the tunnel towards that light of love and warmth. I could feel her slowing down. I could see people that my Mum recognized, and she was delighted to see them. I was calling to her. I was shouting mum, "don't go." It didn't matter mum could not hear me.

The road she was walking on appeared to glow as mum sat down in the dust. I could hear my Mum's thoughts. It was as if Mum knew ahead was good, and love awaited her. However, she didn't want to leave her children or her husband. I heard her think if Harold (my Dad) calls me I am going to turn around and go back down this tunnel.

I headed straight back to my Dad, who was holding her hand and crying. I was saying as loud as I could "call mum, call her now." To my surprise, my Dad didn't react to me at all. He didn't hear me either. However, the man in the white coat put down his hands and said to my Dad, "call her name and keep calling." My Dad looked up at the doctor, and I was shouting yes, "call her, call her now."

Then I was back with my mum, and she was sitting in the dust in the tunnel. I felt her feelings. Mum wasn't scared, just tired, and confused. I could tell by how mum reacted that she recognized the people she could see at the end of the tunnel. I could feel the love flowing from them to her. Then I heard my dad's voice call "Florence" loud and clear. My mum listened to my dad, calling her too. Mum quickly turned and whoosh she was back with my father in her body. My father was crying with relief. The man in the white coat slapped dad on the back and called for the nurses. I then at1256 the speed of light was back in my body on my bed. This is my first memory of what I now know is called astral planing. This ability stayed with me and, is something I have been able to do at will ever since that night.

Chapter One

Cricklade

The next morning, when we got downstairs, my Nana and Grandpa were there with Mrs. White. I was really excited to see them. My brothers were too. My sister was not even a year old, so a little hard to tell how she felt. Susan, my sister, was just cute and lovable with big smiles and happiness. My nana was feeding her, and she looked content to be doing so. Babies do have a way of making everyone happy. Dad was still missing, and the boys were still frantic. I was calm because I had witnessed mum returning to her body. I believed mum was going to be okay.

My brother David was frantic. He was shaking and crying. I don't think he had slept. My brother Grahame was only 6 and a half, he stood silent, just stonily silent. It was eerie looking at them both. I knew they needed to know mum was okay, and I spoke up. I told them mum is better; she went back to her body. They both looked at me, and David scoffed that I would say such a thing. Grahame just ran back to their room as if scalded by a cat. Nana spoke up and told David. Your mum is going to be alright you can stop panicking". David then burst into tears and ran back to their room.

Dad had still not arrived home, and all of us were starting to fret that perhaps things had got worse again. David, who I believed should know more than I did, was pacing and fretting. So even though I had witnessed mum going back to her body, I was starting to worry as well. My Nana was busy getting bags ready and making meals. So I stayed out of the way. I decided to go and play with Susan, entertaining her was fun.

About 4 hours later, my Auntie Hilda and Uncle Charlie arrived. They had driven in from Wellingborough Auntie Hilda was my Nana's sister. Now, remember this is before the telephone had been installed in people's homes. I can only assume that my Father had sent telegrams to my Grandparents. At the time, I don't think I worried about such things. To me, they arrived by magic when they were needed.

My Dad walked in the door at tea time. He looked frazzled, His eyes were red, and his skin was white as a ghost. My Nana, who is my dad's mother, went over and hugged him. Nana had tea on the table, and she told us all to sit down and eat. David started asking questions. David had been so worried also dad still looked so scared. Dad told us all that mum was on the mend and would get better. I wanted to say see, you shouldn't have scoffed at me, but I didn't because even as a young child I intuitively knew not to do that.

Later after my Nana and Aunty Hilda bathed us and got us ready for bed, my Dad called us all into the living room. He looked earnest. Dad explained to us that my Mum might be sick for a while. He needed us to go with our Grandparents and our Aunty Hilda and Uncle Charlie. It was decided that David and I were going to go with Nana and Grandpa to Sunderland. We would stay with them while my Mummy got better. Grahame and Susan would go to Wellingborough with Uncle Charlie and Aunt Hilda.

I still believed my mum was going to be okay because I had seen it all. I went to my dad and hugged him and told him what I had witnessed. Dad acknowledged, the doctor told him to call mum. Mum is going to be alright. She was going to be in the hospital for a while. I know everyone was so relieved. The next morning we set out on the journey north, David and I, stayed away for a long time, I overheard my Nana talking to Grandpa, saying how it was touch and go. I never believed that mum would pass over again. I had been sure that she was back to stay. As more and more time passed, I did start to worry. I may never see her again.

I vividly remember our homecoming, my Grandparents took us by train and then by taxi to get back to the farm. It was a long journey if I went today it would take about 6 hours. At that time it must have been 8 to 9 hours. I can still see myself walking into the house. My mum was making raisin scones my sister was in a pushchair in front of the fire. The radio was on, and a Frank Sinatra song was playing. My brother David raced to my mum, nearly pushing her over, he had the biggest smile ever on his face. He had never believed we would see Mum again. He told me years later that he had witnessed the blood pouring from my mum, and he didn't think they would be able to save her. That he thought, they had separated us, and they weren't going to tell us that she had died. I also know now that we were away for six weeks. To a young child, it felt like a lifetime. I believe that my brother's never recovered from the separation and fear they felt. I understand and witnessed them change who they were. This event opened up my lotus flower and perhaps provoked the psychic sense I was born with to grow.

Chapter Two

The Early Years

By the time I was ready to go to school, we had moved to Alex Farm. It is located 2 miles outside of Cricklade in Wiltshire. Cricklade is a small Saxon village with an ancient history. It has a very mystical feeling, and I would encourage anyone visiting Britain to check out the area. I think of Cricklade as an exceptional place it is located in the heart of the Cotswolds. Close to Stonehenge and the stones of Avery.

Cricklade had given rights to the Romanies (or gypsies as they are widely known) to come and camp there for long periods. They would come to Cricklade every year and stay for months. This privilege was bestowed upon the gypsies by King Charles 1st as they had hidden him from Cromwell's men. They would come and camp for the summer months every year. For a child like myself, this was a perfect place to learn and expand my gift. Cricklade is where I lived until I was fourteen.

The school I attended is in Cricklade itself. St. Samson, is a Church of England school and is located right next door to the church. In those days, religious studies were part of the curriculum. I was fascinated by it all. The whole school would attend the church weekly for services. I felt so close to "spirit" in the church and absorbed the lessons avidly. I loved the words of Jesus, I could feel the words had meaning, and I felt closer and closer to God. I know this is perceived as a strange oxymoron now. Yet at that time, I studied hard the teachings of the bible. I still to this day love to read the teachings of Jesus. My understanding of the scripture may be different than what other people understand. This book may lead you to reach some of the same conclusions I have arrived at.

Next to the church is a graveyard, and as little girls do my friends, and I would wander through the cemetery. I would tell my friend stories about the people buried there. I would hear the whispers, just like I had listened to my mum and dad's thoughts. I would tell my friends what they had been like, how they had died, that sort of thing.

My friends found my "stories" fascinating. They would tell their parents what I had said. Remember this is a small village and generations of people have lived and died there. The whispers I heard would be about relatives and people my friend's parents were either related to or had known. The integrity of my messages became quite widely known. It did not take long for my reputation as having the "gift" to become accepted. Not that I really understood why other people didn't hear what I heard. Or why it was called a gift. To some people, it obviously was not a gift but a curse.

At the age of 11 in the UK, every child was given an exam called the 11 plus. If you did well, you were sent to a grammar school. In my case, after I passed the 11 plus it changed my daily life completely. For starters, the Grammar school was located in Malmesbury. This was 30 miles away from my home. As you can imagine, this posed a problem. We lived 2 miles from Cricklade and 32 miles from the school. The town council met with my parents and me to discuss how to accommodate transportation for myself to get to school. It was agreed that the town would pay for a taxi to pick me up in the morning to take me to the bus stop. Where I would get the bus to the school in Malmesbury, when school was over, I would take the bus back to Cricklade. Father would pick me up when he was done work at 5 pm. This gave me 2 hours every day to spend in Cricklade. I would visit with my friends and of course, find people that would teach me more about what I could see and know.

As a child, you do not understand that other people do not hear and see what you do. I recall seeing cords attaching everyone like spider webs. When someone really liked another person, the silver cord would glow quite brightly. If they did not like the other person, the silver cord would be thin and dull. When anger was involved, the silver cords would vibrate and glow. The angry silver cords felt more powerful even than like. I understood automatically, that anger is a compelling feeling. This has become a basis for my work. To teach my clients to love harder than they hate. To use the power of love and make the cords vibrate. This is also the basis of the teachings of all religions.

As my reputation as a psychic grew, so did my understanding that it was somewhat unique to know the things I did. I also understood that the cords I saw connecting people like cobwebs, no-one else saw. Eventually, I could no longer see them either. I still can sense the silver cords that join us and know what they are saying. It is now a sense rather than a seeing. I think I got fed up with pushing the cobwebs aside. To this day I still sense them and know they are there. I have talked to many people through the years, and some have experienced the silver cords precisely as I did, Others see just the colors and sense the feelings. There is not a wrong way or right way. It is a perception that everyone can have.

Chapter Three

Lily-Rose

Now I had two hours after school five days a week, basically unsupervised, I sought out teachers to help me understand my "gift." It did not take long for me to find one. I was taken under the wing of a wonderful woman named Lily-Rose. Lily-Rose was a gypsy but because of her age, and health, she no longer traveled with the gypsies. So she had settled down in Cricklade in a small cottage close to the Red Lion Pub. My friend Val and I would go to her house. Lily-Rose would tell us stories of the "gift." Lily-Rose spent hours telling us stories of how she had helped people heal, with herbs, and by planting positive seeds. Lily-Rose would read the palms of people and help them to understand who they are and the destiny she would see written in their palms. Lily-Rose was a gift to me, as she taught me how to read and make sense of what I saw and experienced. She taught me to understand the aura's around people, and to discern the colors and the sensations I received. It is as if I can sense the person's soul.

To this day, I can hear her voice guiding me to pay attention to the sensation of color and what it meant when I sensed it. I cannot tell you the joy she gave me. Her teachings are a gift to my clients from Lily-Rose. By sharing so freely of her knowledge, Lily-Rose kept the experience alive. To this day, I read palms the way Lily-Rose taught me. I have read many books on the subject, yet the old method seems to hold true. I do admit that spirit has adjusted with the times now. As the lives we lead today are not as cut and dried as they once were. For example, if the palm indicates two children, this can mean that they are not necessarily your own but come with the person you love. Or you may have an abortion, and that can possibly show up. Marriage can be common law, I may sense this, but the lines in the palm do not tell me this. I have to rely on spirit to clarify the lines and symbols to me, as I said times have changed.

I feel that by visiting Lily-Rose and paying such close attention to her, that we made the last year of her life happier than it would have been. I know she was happy sharing her knowledge. Lily-Rose looked forward to teaching me as much as I loved to learn. I was devastated when I was twelve years old. Lily-Rose passed away. I sensed her going during the night and felt her come to me and touch my cheek. The next morning I was informed she had passed. She was loved by so many people that the funeral was a huge event.

This funeral was a big deal in the gypsy community as Lily-Rose was renowned throughout the land as a psychic, and healer. People of gypsy descent came from far and wide. The funeral was an amazing event, a celebration of the life of a wonderful woman. Every item she had owned was made out of flowers. A procession that stretched for miles lined the streets of Cricklade. The bonfires were lit, and the people danced as I had never seen before, This is an experience I have never forgotten. They celebrated her death as if it was a graduation of her soul. I understand this so much now. As death is just a journey, we still remain.

The lessons I learned from Lily-Rose were so profound that these skills helped me all of my life. As it happens, my niece called her daughter Lily-Rose, and my daughter said that she was upset because she had planned to call her daughter Lily-Rose (if she had one). To the best of my recollection, I never told them about my friend and mentor, Lily-Rose, or mentioned her name. Co-incidence? I think not.

As you already know from my experience at three years old, I never feared death. I saw at the age of three that we go somewhere, and that is a knowing that is so profound, It is this knowledge and knowing that has led me in my life to share and encourage people to live their best lives.

I am, happy to share knowledge of life, spirit, and soul. I want everyone to understand that our souls, that part of ourselves goes to another dimension. We still are us, we still feel, love, and exist in this different dimension.

Chapter Four

Séances

The thing about being psychic is you don't really know what to do with it. So learning to read palms and the aura is a good starting point. Yet knowing there is more information to be had, leads one to experiment with whatever tools you read about. Or it did me anyway.

After Lily-Rose passed, I started to hold seances. Lily-Rose had explained to me how to do it, but I had yet to do one. I wanted to communicate with her so badly. I did not know that ouija boards existed. So I cut up cards and put the alphabet on the cards then I wrote a card with yes on one, and no on the other. I made a circle of these cards then used a water glass in the middle for us to touch and see what would happen I was sure Lily-Rose would come through.

Whenever I would have friends around, I would ask them to have a seance with me. Many times I would communicate with Lily-Rose who explained that the soul does live on. She said that our own understanding is so great when we pass. We get to know all, about the lives that we have lived we get to understand our selves with clarity. The way she explained it is that when we pass over, we see all our lives opened up to us. That way, we know why we have the feelings and fears that we do. She also said that we all get to do a life review where we feel the pain of the people we have hurt. This is a lesson we should all understand. It would make us a lot more careful about other people's feelings. I wonder how long people like Hilter will be feeling the pain they caused. I imagine it will be thousands of years. I believe this life review process is what the bible refers to as hell.

One particular day I had friends over to our house, and as usual, was holding a seance. It was addictive and fascinating to speak to spirits. My friends and I all thought so. It was easy to get people to join me in having seances. One particular Saturday, my father came in for lunch. He kind of scoffed at us for having a seance. He said quite mockingly, I thought. He told us," if this is real, then ask the spirit, what horse is going to win the race at 3pm today?"

Of course, I truly believed in the spirit of Lily-Rose, so I asked the question. To my dad's surprise, the glass spelled out the name Blacksalt. I have to say my dad never gambled so even to hear him ask was kind of a joke. He looked in the paper and said if a horse of that name is running, he will put a bet on him. Well, low and behold, sure enough, a horse was running with that name, but it was a long shot. Like 35 to 1 so my dad got in the car, and drove the 2 miles to Cricklade and placed a bet on Blacksalt.

You all know by now that of course, the horse won. I was so excited until I found out that dad had only bet 1 pound. That's right, a message from spirit and he only wagered 1 pound. When I questioned him, he said well, "it was a long shot." I think the fact that spirit gave us the name of a horse running in the race at 3 pm that day was a bigger long shot. Just a thought.

By the time I was going to Malmesbury grammar school, I was quite well known for my seances. My physics teacher Mr. Jones was very interested in what I was doing. He allowed a group of us girls to use the physics lab during break time to hold seances. Mr. Jones loved to watch, and he was the person that told me I was a medium. He tested us all with instruments as to the energy we were transmitting. I had lots of good experiences and enjoyed doing this a lot. Until one day, spirit spelled out, danger, death, mother, fire. Then the glass rose above the table and shattered. This event frightened my friends and I. Unfortunately; we did not know what spirit was trying to prepare us for.

We found out a week later as one of my friend's mother poured gasoline over herself and lit herself on fire. We were all devastated, by this. For some incomprehensible reason, I felt responsible for this happening to her mother. My friends held me a little responsible too. Of course, I know that I could not have prevented this from happening. My friends thought I should have questioned the spirit further. They were sure that if I had asked for more information, perhaps this tragedy would have been averted. This was my first taste of feeling the weight of the responsibility of the "gift" My friends and I never regained the friendship we once had. This shook me a lot, and I stopped doing seances for a long, long time

Chapter Five

Psychic Tools

In the summer of my 14th, year, my cousin Hazel was getting married. Our whole family went to Wellingborough to attend the wedding. My great uncle Charlie and aunty Hilda lived there along with my cousins and lots of our family. I loved going to Wellingborough. I loved my aunt and uncle, and the rest of the family. This was my first wedding, and it was super fun. While we were there, I walked through the living room while my Uncle Charlie was with a woman, reading her cards. I stopped and stared. He shooed me out of the room. Of course, my parents had shared with the family that I had the gift as they called it. So after the lady left, Uncle Charlie came and got me. He asked me what I saw in the cards which were still laid out. I told him I saw a baby being born. I saw a car accident and many other things. He was quite excited. He questioned me about who had taught me to read cards. I told him I had never been shown how to read any cards. So uncle Charlie began the journey of teaching me to read the playing cards. Now let me explain these were ordinary playing cards. Not tarot or oracle cards just plain playing cards. I had not known that my Uncle Charlie had the gift. It was good to find out that this was a family gift. For some reason, it made me feel more acceptable.

That is how I found out my Great Grandmother, Elizabeth had been a very renowned psychic in Sunderland. A town on the North East coast of Britain. In fact, Elizabeth was often referred to as the witch of Southwick. Apparently, not only did My great Grandmother do readings, but she also made love potions and used herbs to help heal people. She was quite famous as a healer. My uncle Charlie told me about her. Uncle Charlie let me know that I probably inherited the "gift" from her. For her own reasons, when I asked my mother about my great-grandmother, mum told me about her quite reluctantly. As you can imagine, it is not easy to have a psychic daughter. I am sure my mum did not want me to get wrapped up in this path, as she wanted me to live a 'regular' (whatever that is) life.

However, reluctantly mum relayed one of the following stories about my great grandmother. I am sure she told me this as a lesson to learn about the dangers and responsibility of readings etcetera. My grandmother Jane was my great grandmother's granddaughter. Jane and her friend Stacy had a psychic reading from her. Stacey was only 16 years old. My Great Grandmother gave her lots of information that happened. Stacey was a true believer. So Stacy believed everything Elizabeth told her. Well, unfortunately, She told Stacy that she would die at the age of 55. So all of Stacy's life she repeated she would die at 55. All through her own life, my mum would hear about everything that my Great grandmother, had predicted coming true. As it happens Stacey passed away on her 55th birthday, she just dropped dead. Nothing wrong with her, no symptoms of anything. So my mother believed that it was a seed planted all those years ago by my great grandmother. I was warned to be careful of the seeds you plant. This gift comes with great responsibility. I very rarely tell people if I see death. Spirit has to really insist I share the information before I do so. I understand that mum may have been telling me a story. Yet I do know that it is possible to plant seeds. You will read more about this later on.

Chapter Six

Sunderland

Not long after the wedding in Wellingborough, my father resigned from Alex Farm and moved my sister and myself to Sunderland. My brothers stayed where they were as David was married. He had a young son named Paul, and his wife Gina. They decided to stay in Cricklade. Grahame was in college. Sunderland is where our family is from originally. So we had aunts and uncles, cousins, and grandparents all around us. I loved living there. It's on the coast of the British Channel and very interesting. Sunderland had been one of the biggest shipbuilding cities in the world until after world war 2. You can still see the damage the bombs have done to the City. The Germans would drop the last of their missiles on

Sunderland. before they crossed back to Germany. The scars of destroyed buildings were everywhere. Mum had a scar on her face. This is where a sniper had caught her, with his bullets as she walked home from work. To think I would never had been born or any of my siblings had that sniper not been chased off by a British plane.

On this Sunday, we were all going to have lunch with my Great Aunty Hilda. Aunty Hilda was my grandfather's sister. I had not met her before. It was a lovely day. I remember she made all kinds of salads and desserts. The family was all sitting at the table having our lunch, and suddenly I saw a young man clad in a uniform standing beside my aunt. The man's uniform was an old fashioned RAF uniform. The man looked about 18 years old. I could see him clear as day. He spoke to me and said: "tell my mum I loved flying." Now you have to understand this was new for me. I had heard whispers, but I could actually see this man clear as day. He had red hair and was good looking and not very tall. He told me his name was Tommy. He informed of his death in the battle of Britain in 1943. So at this time, he had been dead twenty-five years. Tommy was so excited that I could see him and hear him, He wanted me to tell Aunty Hilda, who was his mum that he was doing really well. His dad Arthur was also with him. Arthur had reunited with Tommy when he had died nine years earlier. Tommy didn't regret fighting in the war. His only regret was his mother and father's heartache. He told me to tell her, "life goes on, and he loves her." I was so surprised by the vividness of his appearance that I blurted it out to my aunt and everyone else at the table with us.

Yes, that's right, I just blurted it all out. My aunt was taken off guard and teared up. My mum asked my dad to take my sister outside. After he left with Susan, My aunt and mum sat me down and asked me what I saw. I told my aunt what I saw and heard. Tommy was still there I could see him. Tommy was so very pleased. I was telling his mum that he was happy. Aunty Hilda was tearful, and I started to feel awful. She brought out an album and showed me pictures of Tommy, and he was precisely the man standing in the room. After we talked for a while, I understood that I had given my Aunt a gift. I had not understood how much it would mean to a person to know that your loved ones live on. I assumed that everyone knew that. After all, even in the church, we are taught that the soul lives on. More about this later.

Chapter Seven

Monkwearmouth Grammar School

Now I have to go to a new school. It is called Monkwearmouth grammar school. This is the same school my father attended. Years later, my daughter went to this school. My parents had rented a house quite a distance from the school. As the school is not far from my Nana's house, I stayed with my Nana during the week.

I was so nervous about going to a new school. I didn't know anyone that went to this school. At least in Cricklade when I went to Malmesbury, there were kids I knew in the village that went there. It's hard to go to a new school with a different accent and not to know anyone. For your information in Sunderland, the dialect is geordie. I found it really hard to understand what people were saying. People also found it hard to understand my accent from Wiltshire. It really was in those days as if we spoke totally different languages. So I felt like a fish out of water. It was very distressing to be in a different school where you don't understand their speech. So I went to my Uncle Micky and asked if I could spend some time with him. He had the broadest Geordie accent I have ever heard. It became fun to listen to him talk and figure out what he meant. "away man let's go o'er the toon" or have you seen the spuggies in the school sputes" were two of the sentences that always made me laugh out loud. It didn't take me long to get my ears adjusted after that.

I started school and soon made some friends. I was settling in quite nicely. I enjoyed having relatives and cousins around. It felt quite quickly that I belonged here. I loved living beside the sea. The sound and smells are intoxicating to me. I asked Judith Robinson, a school friend, to take me to Southwick. I wanted to visit the area where my Great-Great-Grandmother had lived. When we arrived in Southwick, it felt as if I knew the place so well. I began to wonder if I was the re-incarnation of my great-great-grandmother. Nothing had changed. As we walked around, I recognized the streets and had a strong feeling of Deja Vue. Today I am sure that I have the same soul as my great great grandmother. This, of course, is not provable. However, as you read on, you will perhaps come to believe this as well.

As I explained earlier, I was not holding seances or anything like that anymore. I did, however, take great pleasure in reading peoples aura and reading palms. I had not held a seance or anything like that since the incident with the glass shattering, followed by my friend's mum dying. As I told my new friends about the experiences with the glass, they became excited to do this with me. So as all teenage girls do, I wanted to impress my new friends. The girls wanted to hold seances with me. So I started again, communicating through the glass. It felt so natural to pick up the glass once again and talk to spirit.

My "gift" had increased. I could feel the surge of electricity through my fingers as the glass would hover over the table. The spirit was closer, and it felt at home with me here. I would ask the questions my friends wanted answers to. I would also allow the spirit just to speak. Or should I say spell? I would give answers as asked. Julie, one of my friend's mother, was warned she had breast cancer. Julie went home and insisted her mother get checked. When the tests came back positive, my reputation spread. It was quite good for me to have that kind of validation. I had felt responsible erroneously for a death. This time I had helped save a life. That was the best feeling in the world.

One of the most unusual seances was about myself. I never asked questions for myself. As one of the rules I had been told is to use the gift for others. I had been told if you use it with self-interest, you will lose it. I certainly did not want to lose the "gift." Even at the age of 16, I knew the reward of being able to help others with this "gift" I had. So the two years I spent in Sunderland, I read palms, and held seances and explored everything spiritual.

One particular day my friends and I were holding a seance the spirit was answering questions, like who would we marry? How many GCE's would each of us get. How many children would we have etcetera? Spirit answered each of my friends, and now 50 years later, I discovered through Facebook of all things, that everything has happened as the spirit had said. For myself, spirit said I would not get any GCE's, which are the final exams we take to graduate high school. This was crazy as it was only weeks till we would take the exams. It made no sense that I would not pass any of the exams. Spirit explained that I was going to go to Canada. Now my dad had talked about wanting to move to Canada, but it had all fallen through. Spirit also said that I would marry a man with initials HP, with no middle name. Spirit also kept saying " poor baby," "Poor Baby." I doubted this seance, going to Canada had been canceled. I decided that this spirit was wrong. Even if my Dad decided to go to Canada, I would not go.

Two weeks later, my dad announced we were going to Canada. I was to go with them, and they would not allow me to stay behind and finish school. My parents believed if they let me stay in the UK, I would never leave. Of course, they were right; It was a huge thing to expect me to abandon my life in the UK, especially just before my final exams. In my mind to take me away just before these exams seemed nothing short of unjust. Yet I had been told this would happen and was not given a choice in the matter as by then I was only 16. I was distraught to leave Sunderland and my Nana. I wanted to stay with my nan. I rebelled against the move as much as I could, but my parents promised if I was unhappy when I turned 18. They would pay for me to return to

Sunderland. So I packed my bags and decided to look at this as an adventure.

Chapter Eight

Canada

In those days to immigrate to Canada was point-based. Two years earlier had passed all the exams and had our shots. The job that my father had been offered two years earlier had fallen through. So we had made ourselves comfortable in Sunderland. My mother was delighted as her sisters lived in Sunderland as well as her parents. So for Mum, this was home. Susan and I loved it there as well. Susan was doing great in school. My brother David had followed us up to Sunderland, with his wife, and child. His son Paul was only a year old, and Susan was enthralled with Paul. It was a lovely family time for us.

Imagine all of our disappointment when my father received the call offering him a position in Canada. We talked for hours about it. I understood that this was my father's dream. He felt Canada was the land of milk and honey. So eventually we reconciled that we had to move to Canada. My mum talked to all of us and said dad had to have his chance to live his dream.

We were sent to Springbank in Ontario. My dad was to manage a farm there. Springbank is a tiny farming community. Springbank is located between Belleville and Madoc. Springbank is basically just a few farms and a small store to get odds and ends. Imagine our shock to see worms in the bathwater. The house we were given to live in was on well water, and the well needed to be refilled so at the bottom of the well there were worms. EEK.. It was quite disconcerting. My friends in England had filled my head with stories of the wild west. My parents wanted me to go to school as I had not graduated. (their fault). Also, because in Ontario, the kids went to school till they were 18. My parents wanted me to make friends and get to graduate in Canada. Susan, of course, had to go to school as she was only 13. So the decision was made I would go to school.

The School I attended is called Centre Hasting Secondary School. My sister Susan went to junior high. On the first day at school, I wore a skirt and shirt, and tie. As in England, we wore uniforms to school. This uniform is a skirt and socks and then on top a button-up dress shirt with a jumper (sweater) and a tie. I had no idea that in Canada, they did not wear uniforms. When I arrived, almost everyone was dressed in jeans and T-shirts (a modern-day uniform so to speak) As you can imagine I looked out of place. Apparently, the kids thought I was a teacher.

The first person to befriend me was a young man called Dennis. He followed me everywhere and made sure I got to class. He was the head boy of the school, so I thought it was kind of his job to show me around. I learned shortly after. It wasn't actually his job.

By this time I figured out he liked me. He didn't hide it very well. Dennis would bring me beautiful little things to school. Dennis soon asked me to go meet his parents. They were extraordinary people. I came to love them very much. Dennis's mother Grace was tall and slim. Grace was a person filled with fun and happiness. His dad Percy was short and overweight, yet his personality was compelling. He was president of the legion and worked at the mines. Even though they looked like an odd couple, they were amazing together.

I will never forget Grace, looking at me and reacting so stunned. She reached into a drawer and pulled out a sketch of a girl that looked a lot like me. I asked who is this, and she said Dennis had sketched it months ago, He had told his mum this girl is coming into my life, I will love her. We did love each other; the connection was and is fantastic. Dennis could sit at one end of a room and look at cards. I would tell people what cards he was looking at. A great party trick as you can imagine. I would finish his sentences. He would finish mine. At times it felt as if we were one person. We had an extraordinary connection that has lasted to this day.

Chapter Nine

Maple Arbour Farm

My dad was not happy in Springbank as the wages were so low, He answered an ad for a partnership on a farm near Brantford Ontario. I remember clear as day, going for the job interview. My mum, dad and Susan and I went to the meeting. The lady Helen Howell that owned the farm wanted to meet us all. We would be living in the same house as her. Not in the same quarter but still in the same house. I had a very eerie feeling when we went to the house. I told mum that I did not like the place. Of course, I understand that mum probably thought it was about moving again. I did not go into detail. The place just felt off. I couldn't explain why. However The interview went well, and my father prepared to move us all to Maple Arbour Farm. You can imagine I rebelled mightily. I was used to the school now. I had friends and Dennis, I did not and would not change schools again.

This time my parents agreed that as it was only nine months to graduation. They allowed me to stay with a friend in Madoc. My friend, Judy's mother, decided to let me live with them. My parents would not allow me to stay with Dennis. That was fine with me. During breaks and holidays, I would go to Maple Arbour Farm sometimes Dennis would come with me.

Whenever I stayed at the farm, I would hear footsteps walking around in the residence of Helen Howell, the owner of the farm. I asked my mum, dad, and Susan if they heard them too. Of course, they verified that they did. The noise was loud and clear. All of us would all know Helen was out or away. So clearly they weren't her footsteps. We would hear cupboards open and close. My mother would make comments like " poor woman she doesn't know she's dead." We knew it was a woman, that's without her even showing herself. We could tell she was female, by the footsteps and the way she would sound busy in the kitchen. We would go over to her side of the house many times to see if anyone was there. No-one was ever there.

Eventually, I did see a tall woman in an old fashioned dress with a pinafore on. She was very faint though, in fact, quite translucent. She was looking for something or someone. When she saw me watching her, she became agitated and waved me away as if I was an intruder. She looked frightened to see me. I asked her who she was, but she wasn't talkative like Tommy had been. The woman just disappeared from my sight as I tried to question her. After a bit, we all just accepted that the house is haunted.

One night as I lay in my bed, I saw an apparition of a young girl. She appeared to be about 11 years old. She was nodding her head no. I asked her what she wanted? The young girl was not frightened neither was I. The little girl was wearing a long nightie she was obviously distressed. She just pointed and kept nodding no! I knew by this time that if a ghost or apparition appears to you that you should absolutely pay attention. I distinctly felt that this little girl was trying to warn me of impending doom. I know that when ghosts are giving you a message or even a warning, you need to listen. It takes a lot of effort for them to show themselves, so pay attention. I told my parents and Susan about this vision. Susan said she had sensed her presence as well. We did not listen to the warning in part because dad loved the farm.

One of my greatest regrets is I didn't demand that we get off this farm.

As it happens my sister Susan adored Dennis, they got along really well. It had been trying for Susan, to adjust to all the moves. Susan had been best friends with my brother David and had loved Paul. So the year I was away at school, my brothers still in England was a difficult time for her. So when she graduated Junior High, she asked if Dennis would to take her to the prom. I was so happy that he did that for her. I knew how tough she was finding adjusting to another new school. I really appreciated Dennis taking her to her prom. They had a great time at the dance and Dennis helped her break into the cliques that form in schools.

Once again, I found myself in a new town with no friends. Susan was glad to have me home, mainly because I had learned to drive. So even though Susan was 2 and a half years younger than me, we became close again. I got a part-time job working at Woolco and bought a car to get around in. My sister loved having me home as it meant more ability to get out and about. As I was driving now, we could go into town and see movies, or go to the drive-ins which were abundant at that time. Or just go to the mall.

Unlike myself, Susan loved farm life. Susan loved animals; they were her very favorite things in the world. Quite often, Susan would help my dad on the farm. She would bring along her dog Sparky, a border collie and they would make themselves useful, they would round up the cows. Susan learned to drive the tractors and would help dad with the bailing. Susan seemed to fit right in on the farm. After school, the first thing she would do is go and play with Sparky. She was very athletic and bright. Then the worst thing you can imagine happened. I was going with friends to Tukey Point. It's about an hour away from Brantford. Susan asked if she could come with me. Unfortunately and to my great regret, I said no as we were going on my friend's motorbike.

My friend Warren and I arrived at Turkey Point, where he had a trailer and a boat. We went out in the boat and were going to water ski. Suddenly I felt sick to my stomach and insisted we go back to Brantford. Warren was upset as we had planned to stay for a few days. I explained that I had a terrible feeling and needed to get back home. Warren was well aware of my "gift" as he had seen me do many readings for people. So instead of getting upset with me, he took my back to Brantford,

I will never forget riding in the car to drive two miles to the farm. I had the radio on and turned it off. I had a sense of impending doom. When I arrived back at the farm, my mother came running out of the house and said: "Susan is dead." I swear I nearly hit her. I don't know why that was the reaction, but it was. It turns out my sister was putting the tractor away, and she had apparently popped the clutch on the tractor. The Barn was on a slight hill, so the tractor flipped over. Susan died instantly with a broken neck. If I had not turned off the radio, I would have heard the announcement on my way to the farm. I doubt I would have been able to drive the rest of the way. I also could have caused an accident. I do believe my angels protected me.

My mother fell apart at the loss of her youngest daughter, My father was also devastated. My father blamed himself for allowing Susan to drive the tractors, my mother, unfortunately, felt the same way. My father retired to the barn, and my mother stayed in bed. I had to step up and see to the funeral arrangements and spend time at the funeral home for the viewing. My brother Grahame flew over from England. He was a great support to me at that time. The loss of Susan was horrendous. Even though I know, she is still with us in spirit. We all miss her terribly.

Three nights after my sister passed over; I went to my bedroom to try to sleep. I saw my sister sitting on the edge of my bed. I said to her, "I see you, I know this is real." We talked a lot, Susan told me that she was happy and it is beautiful on the other side. She said our grandpa was there and lots of other people that she hadn't known. Susan said they had a welcoming party for her, and it was great. It made sense because the only person that we had that had died was our grandpa. Susan told me to think to myself that she had got to graduate before me. She said that death is a graduation. The way she described being on the other side is like the mirror in a police station. Susan can see us all. Not many people can see her except for people that have this extra sense like me.

We talked about what it feels like being light Susan said you still feel like yourself. Susan described the tunnel that I had already seen; she also described doing her life review, Susan, told me that for her, this review was quite quick because she was so young. She said you feel all the pain that you cause other people in this life and you experience it as your own pain as you pass on. I have always remembered this. It is so much a part of my belief system that I am sure to be mindful of how I treat others. In fact, knowing this, I have to say it makes me a better person. I always try to be kind, no matter what. However, this can also cause problems because I tended to be selfless, which is not good either. It has taken me years to learn how to navigate this knowledge. In other words, my feelings matter too. For example, a person should not stay in an unhealthy marriage to avoid hurting the other person.

Susan wanted me to explain to mum and dad that she was happy, but their grief pained her. Even when we pass the cords that connect us are still intact so as my parents grieved. Susan's cords were picking up the pain of their feelings. This led me to understand that when we die the emotions, we have also go with us. I understood what Susan was saying but wondered how I could convince mum and dad that you have just graduated too early? Susan told me that Sparky her dog, would come to me in the morning and sit on my knee. We laughed together; we both knew mum and dad would believe me. Sparky always ignored my existence. Susan told me she could bring him to me. That will be easy, the animals still see us, she said.

The next morning when I got up, my dad was in the kitchen, my mum was in bed. I took the opportunity to tell dad what I experienced the night before and what Susan had told me. Together we went outside. Now the barn is about a city block from the house. Sparky was over at the barn right where Susan had turned the tractor over. When he saw me, he ran over and climbed up on to my knee. My father was crying. He said: "good enough for me." He went upstairs and shared with my mother what had occurred. My mum was in far too much grief to absorb what had happened. Three days later, after Sparky had sat on my knee, he disappeared never to be seen again. I sincerely believe he went to be with my sister.

A month after the funeral, my mother traveled to Springbank to visit Claire was a friend of my mother. They had met each other when we had lived in Springbank. When mum arrived at Claire's, she walked into the house. Claire immediately turned to my mum and said: "By the way, I saw Susan last night, she was so happy running in the fields with her dog"! Well, the dams broke open. My mother just sat and cried. Claire apologized over and over again. Mum told her "Thank You I needed to hear that," afterward it was as if mum sincerely knew Susan is happy where she is.

Chapter Ten

The Onandaga United Church.

After Susan's funeral, we as a family decided to get grief counselling at the church. We asked the minister if it was possible to get together with us once a week, for a month. As a family, this was an excellent decision for our healing and growth. Tom Vandershaf was the new minister at the church; I felt he was so welcoming and very helpful in the healing process. Personally, I was so interested in spirit that I soaked up everything Tom talked about. Tom taught me about love. It was not romantic love Tom spoke of; instead, he spoke on the love of Christ. He often talked about the bible as a guide for our lives. I started going every week to service. I was soaking up everything the Church had to teach. I had the idea of getting people together with us and wanted to include my parents. I discussed with my mum and dad about launching a bible study group with Tom. They agreed that this was a great idea. Everywhere I went, I would talk about the Love of Christ, and I glowed with joy. At one of the bible studies, a new person Debbie from the village came. While we were talking, she mentioned that every family that had lived in Maple Arbour Farm had lost their youngest child.

This was very distressing to us all. My mother said had she had that information. We would never have moved here. It made sense of the little girl I had seen and why she had appeared to us. Even Helen, the owner of the farm, had lost her little sister. Helen's sister had contracted meningitis and had passed overnight. The people that had worked on the farm before my father had lost there youngest daughter. Their little girl had wandered onto the train tracks and been hit by a train. That in itself was very peculiar as the train only ran past the farm twice a day. It ran at Noon and 11 pm. The original house built on Maple Arbour Farm. Burnt to the ground, the youngest daughter had perished in the fire.

At one point, I had 32 young women and men attend this little church in Onandaga. The people in the village were astounded and thrilled to see the Church so vibrant. I had Tom help me to reconcile my "gift" with the teachings of Christ. He explained that all through the bible, there were wise men. These men and women are significant figures. Tom helped me reconcile my "gift" as a gift of the holy spirit. Tom motivated me to want to become a minister myself. The church council-sponsored me to university to become a minister. I would be one of the first female ministers in the United Church.

I became so filled with the gift that I insisted on being baptized in water. I wanted a full immersion baptism. My friends also wanted to participate in a full baptism service. So as it happens, my father had installed a full-size swimming pool at the farm. He was in complete agreement with us to use the pool to hold these baptisms. So on a beautiful September evening, we all gathered at Maple Arbour Farm. There were about 25 of us. Our minister Tom was there in a long robe which he wore into the pool. The lights were on around the pool. There were five of us being baptized. We were so excited and the energy was buzzing with excitement.

All of us had on our swimsuits with a robe over us. My friend Warren had a polaroid instant camera. We all listened as Tom talked about the sanctity of baptism, and washing away our sins. It was marvellous for me to look around and see all the happiness that was present. Each of us became baptized, Warren took pictures with the Polaroid camera that instantly developed the photo's The holy spirit was visible like flames with a dove in the middle of the wings, descending on Marilyn. This photo amazed all of us. Warren had said he needed a sign to believe that the holy spirit or Jesus and God existed. I insisted this was, of course, a sign. My father was thrilled. Dad had filled with the holy spirit himself. Dad sent the photo to Polaroid to make sure it was not a fault in the film. Of course, it wasn't defective. The holy spirit had descended on us that night and revealed itself to us.

Afterward, the gifts started to reveal themselves. Marilyn was so filled with love. To all of our pleasure, she was able to play guitar. Marilyn also found that she could learn languages with ease. Tom pointed out that these were mentioned in the bible. There are some of the gifts of the holy spirit. Marilyn became a missionary and has traveled the world, helping the needy. Joan, one of my dear friends, decided to go to bible college, where she met her husband. Their lives have been an example to so many as they fostered children, as well as raised their own. My friends were all blessed in unimaginable degrees. They have all made a difference in their corner of the world.

Chapter Eleven

Healing

My mother and father healed their hearts. Never completely as the loss of a child is horrific. Through the bible studies and seeing God in action, they became more at peace with what had happened. This was never more prevalent than when a friend of my mother was involved in a terrible car accident. Her daughter Janice was on placed life support. The Dr's said that if she lived, the damage would be extensive. Tom and our group started a prayer vigil for Janice. We prayed with absolute faith that Janice would live and be healed. By this time, the power of faith was an absolute belief. As big and small, our group had experienced miracles. The prayer vigil lasted for days. There was never a moment that less than 4 of us would pray for Janice. We took it in turns round the clock the prayers were sent up to God. On the 5th day, Janice was taken off life support, the doctors held out no hope and expected her to pass. I didn't believe for one minute that our prayers would not be answered. I could not and would not allow doubt in my mind.

Janice came round as the anesthetic wore off. She was breathing on her own. In itself a miracle. As the days went by we all continued to pray. We did not want her to be brain damaged or crippled. By now, the whole church was watching and praying for complete healing for Janice. It wasn't like she jumped out of bed and started running around. Don't get me wrong there was still healing to be done. By the end of the month, Janice had all her faculties intact. I am happy to report Janice went on to have a happy life without any handicaps. Many more miracles occurred, it was a wonderful time for me,

Having the gift of medium ship and having embraced my psychic self. It was not easy to be surrounded by other students of the bible. They all frowned so heavily upon me. I was not understood, as Tom had understood me. I felt like a pariah. I will never forget one of the students bringing a large cross to class. He went to the professor and asked him to demonstrate an exorcism on me.

I didn't stay with the church, as I had a conflict between accepting my gift as from God, and what the narrow-minded people I became surrounded with, thought about it. You can imagine I never asked for the sight I had. I was born with this "gift" it isn't a choice; it is just there. How could I repudiate this? I believed that the church was too set in dogma. The more I studied, the more I needed to leave. Not because of belief but because I identified with the word of God, not man. You will learn more about this as I continue.

Chapter Twelve

Kitchener

So through the years, the ability I was gifted with has been used to help people in their lives. I married the man HP as I just mentioned. We lived in Kitchener Waterloo. A very vibrant town. I was working at the Waterloo Motor Inn and was studying business. We had many friends in Kitchener. I was expecting our first child. I was 28 weeks pregnant. On a Friday night, our friends Cheryl and Leo came over for supper, and to play cards. Before they left Cheryl asked me to do a psychic reading and layout her cards.

As I laid out the cards, I saw Cheryl, and Leo going on a trip. They were going to Windsor to visit her family the next day. I told them they had to be very careful as I saw death and a near-death. Cheryl asked if it was her and Leo I said no because she would hear about it from someone with dark hair that she did not know very well. I said a lot more, but this is the primary gist of this reading.

That night after they left, Helmut and I went to bed. I woke up about 5 AM screaming with pain. Helmut called the doctor who stated it was probably Braxton Hicks contractions and I should take a bath. As instructed, I took a bath. The pain intensified. I was screaming in pain. I was vomiting and started to bleed. Helmut called back the doctor who told us to rush to the hospital where he would meet us.

By the time we got to the hospital, I was freezing cold. I had lost a lot of blood. My doctor met us there, he gave me a shot of morphine, and a nurse wrapped me in warm blankets. I was so cold. I was still screaming with pain. To this day, I remember the nurse saying you must have a low threshold of pain. (I wanted to punch her) I found out later I was in hard labor. They rushed me into the theatre. The anesthetist started the countdown. Now it was my turn to travel the tunnel that I had visited before, with my mother.

I could see the doctors working on me. It was as if I was looking down on them I could see the staff as they rushed around me. The blood continued to pour out of me. Then whoosh, I am in the tunnel that beautiful warm tunnel it was so dusty. I could see my sister and my grandpa and other people that I did not know. I did recognize they were family. I was not scared. I wanted to talk to my sister so much. I was trying to run towards her. Susan was yelling at me, "not yet" "go back," turn around." I resisted leaving the tunnel. It felt lovely here, and I wanted to visit everyone. Without making a choice, I was back out of the tunnel. I hadn't chosen to leave but had just shifted into another space. I was out of the tunnel but not in my body, I watched as the doctors performed a c-section. I saw my baby boy so beautiful but lifeless. I heard the doctor as he said my baby had drowned in my blood. I was so sad I was crying as I watched the doctors work. It looked hopeless. I was ready to return to the tunnel. I was prepared to go to my sister. I felt myself floating in a sea of pain so emotional. I was praying for my parents as I knew they would be devastated to lose me. I could actually feel their pain.

I heard the doctor ask the nurse to go and speak to Helmut. I couldn't hear what he was saying. I

followed the nurse as she left the operating room.
I could see Helmut outside in the hall, Helmut e
was on a stretcher. Apparently, he had fainted, the
nurse was giving him a cookie and juice. The
nurse I was following went and spoke to him. She
asked him if they could use plasma to stop the
bleeding. The nurse explained it was
experimental, but basically the only hope they
had. The blood was just running through me. I
had seen the blood pouring out of me. I wondered
to myself if they could save me. Susan had said:
"not yet." did that mean I was going to stay here.
I did not know. I wasn't certain I wanted to stay.
Helmut agreed with the nurse and signed
something. I followed the nurse back into the
operating room. I watched as they put a bag on
the stand and attached it to me. I heard a nurse
ask if they were going to perform a hysterectomy.
The doctor said not he could help it. I was
watching the doctor and all the people around me
work. I was crying and praying. I realized I
wanted to stay. I wanted to have children. I was
praying the doctor would save my uterus.

Then nothing, I do not remember re-entering my
body. I just woke up in recovery. My Dad was
with me holding my hand. My Mum was in
Britain visiting her mum and relatives, so it was
my dad who came to be with me. He explained

that this was what had happened to mum all those years ago. Mum had also had a placenta abruption.

I found out later that I would have died if plasma had not been newly discovered. The doctor who used this was one of a few that knew about plasma, and that it was available in the hospital. I was told by my nurse as I recovered that I was a miracle. Had another doctor answered the call that morning, I would have probably died. I would definitely have lost my ability to have children. His name was Doctor Sel To this day; I give thanks for his caring and skill. My nurse shared with me any other doctor would have performed a hysterectomy to try to stop the bleeding. My placenta had ripped away from the lining of the uterus. This is known as a placenta abruption. They told me it was a 1 in a million, event and would never happen again. Yet it had happened to my mother.

As you all know in the 70's mobile phones were not part of our lives. Not many of us even used answering machines. Voice mail was not an option offered on residential telephones. Helmut nor I knew Cheryl's parent's contact info. So Helmut had no way of contacting Cheryl. Letting her know about the recent events and that I was in the hospital. Cheryl and Leo returned to Kitchener after the weekend. Cheryl went to pick up some groceries and ran into a girl that I worked with called Laura. Laura did not know Cheryl very well but recognized her as my friend. Laura asked Cheryl how I was doing? Cheryl said I was doing well she had dinner with us on Friday, Laura responded with oh you haven't heard then? Laura then told Cheryl what had happened. Cheryl was in disbelief as everything I had predicted in her reading, had been about myself. Cheryl immediately came to the hospital and helped me so much to get back on my feet.

We talked about how the reading I had done for her was so accurate. Neither of us had thought it to be about myself. When a couple of years later, Cheryl was expecting a child and started to have a placenta abruption. She recognized the symptoms immediately. I had explained how the baby had begun to move quickly and how it had felt. Cheryl knew what was happening to her was what had happened to me. (I had described everything in full gory detail). Her husband rushed her to the hospital. Her little boy lived and now is an exceptionally, beautiful human being.

Minchinhampton 1955 - 1959

Cricklade 1959 - 1969

St. Samson Church, Cricklade

Sunderland 1969 - 1971

Maple Arbour Farm 1973 - 1976

Onandaga, Maple Arbour Farm

Kitchener, Ontario 1976 - 1978

Calgary 1978 - Present

Calgary 1978 - Present

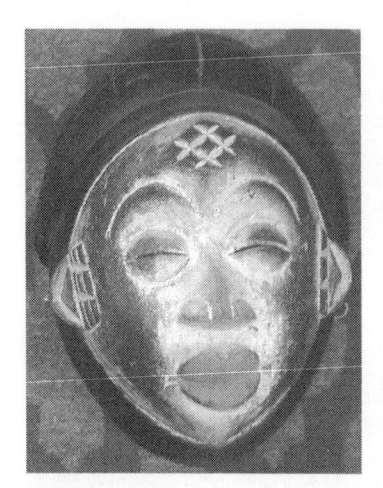

Voodo Masks ~ Haunted House

Your True Body

- Soul
- Body
- Emotional Body
- Spiritual Body

© Psychic Medium Judy

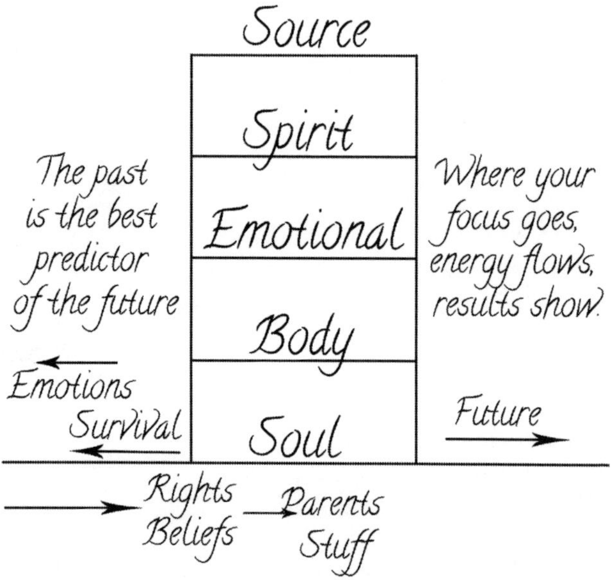
Source
Spirit
Emotional
Body
Soul
The past is the best predictor of the future
Where your focus goes, energy flows, results show.
Emotions
Survival
Future
Rights Beliefs
Parents Stuff

Sacred Ladder

© Psychic Medium Judy

Chapter Thirteen

Calgary

After losing my child, I wanted to get away from Kitchener. My brother David had moved to Calgary, David wanted Helmut and I to move there. David convinced Helmut that Calgary would be better for us. In February of 1978, we packed up and drove to Calgary.

After we moved to Calgary, we lived with my brother for a year. We succeeded in having two children, a daughter, and a son. We worked hard. Life threw us many challenges. I continued to do readings for people regularly. I had a reputation for accuracy. I knew I needed to learn more, how to help people. For me, it was not enough to know what the problems are. I needed to help make my client's lives better. I studied as many healing modalities as I could. I studied everything about people that I could find.

Calgary has a special energy. Calgary always feels as if lots is happening. I felt a connection to the city as soon as we arrived. I had my daughter in 1981 so my mum and dad came to visit us. They felt good in Calgary. My mother hated the farm now and convinced my dad to sell up and move to Calgary as well. It was great to have them here. It gave my daughter and mum lots of special time with each other as I went back to work.

My Nana was still alive and living in Sunderland. There was only mail to communicate. My Nana resisted having a phone. Eventually, my mum and dad returned to the UK, to look after my Nana who lived until she was 96. My daughter followed them. I always say my parents beat me up to get me to Canada. Then they left me here. LOL. It was 30 years later. My son was born in 1983 and is still here in Calgary.

I never considered using my gift as a source of income. I had never charged for my readings. I would only accept donations. Then my mum died. At the same time, my son had a breakdown. I had no idea this would be the best thing that ever happened to me. My mother went to work for me from the moment she passed. I could feel her talking to my angels. I know it was my mum guiding me. My son was hospitalized and was in terrible distress. My finances were destroyed. In the end, I had no idea what I was to do now. I couldn't continue with our business. My son had been pivotal in our company. Without my son, it was impossible to maintain.

Chapter Fourteen

New Age Books, & Crystals

I trust spirit, I have been shown that if you listen, your angels will guide you. I did what Lily-Rose had taught me so many years before. I wrote my dilemma on a piece of paper and put it under my pillow. Whatever thought is in my mind in the morning, I act upon it. I was at my wit's end. I asked my angels that night what path I should take? The answer in the morning was obvious. Go to New Age Books & Crystals.
I knew they were telling me to open myself to working as a psychic medium.

I listened, this was a Tuesday morning. I got up and drove to New Age Books & Crystals. I knew where it was as I had frequently bought books there. I arrived at 10:30AM and was surprised to see the store was closed. (what retail store doesn't open till 11AM) I could see someone walking around inside the building. I was positive I was supposed to be here.

I felt so nervous this was a real test. I knocked on the door, and a young man answered. It turns out that if I had gone any other day, Yvan would not have been there as Tuesday is the only day he worked. He was the new owner as his father had retired. I told him who I was and what I did. He asked me to do a reading for him. His mother came through loud and clear. Barb, Yvan's mother, had died a couple of years before. Barb told me that she had initially started the book store. She told her son that she was always there for him. She told him through the medium ship that he was doing a good job keeping the store going. When I finished his reading, he confirmed that he would be happy to give me recommendations. He said he had enough psychics at the store and didn't have room for me. I left feeling, let down as I was so confident that my angels were right.

When I retired that night, I asked my angels the same question again. I wrote it on my paper and put it under my pillow. In the morning, I heard my angels, "Oh ye of little faith." So I was sure that I just had to trust that I was going to be taken care of. That Yvan would recommend me to the right person. On Friday, Yvan called and offered me the basement in the store to work out of. It was disgustingly dirty. The stairs needed replacing. The bathroom had to be refurbished. All the dirt had had to be cleared away and walls built. It was a challenge I was up to. My angels had said this was where I should be. I was not going to disobey or doubt them.

I got to work my friends helped me get the place ready, within a week I was able to have clients come to me there. It took about three months to complete everything. So I had fashioned a small space I could work in as the renovations were completed. This arrangement worked well for Yvan and me. The store was busier because I brought traffic. I was busier because of the traffic in the store. My reputation grew, my business flourished. This lasted for two years. Then things changed, the store that was sharing the rent with New Age moved out. Yvan decided that he would turn the vacant space into a psychic den, and keep the book store. Yvan was going to transform the "New Age." I was not aware of this as I was not part of the decisions I was a tenant.

On a Friday in October 2014, David, the manager of the store, told me about this change that was going to happen. He advised me to find another space. I was distraught and scared. I relied on my income to support myself and my son. After David went upstairs, I packed up to leave. I was meeting Mel, a friend of mine at a coffee shop across the road from the store. Mel is a property manager, but I was just meeting him for coffee I had only just heard I would need to leave, As it happens Mel was on the phone when I walked in the cafe. He apologized, he couldn't stay for coffee. Mel had to go up to one of the properties he looked after in the North East of Calgary. Mel invited me to go with him, which I did. I needed to vent about losing my space, ask his advice as to whether I should try to stay with the changes, or find another place.

My angels were telling me that Yvan wanted me to leave as I would not fit in with his plans. The whole basement was all mine, I had paid for all the renovations and built two rooms, one for readings and one for meditations and crystal healing. I was sure Yvan wanted the space I had created. I understood that I would not fit in. I would not help his new business model. I would be a deterrent. The new psychics would have to compete with me. I was paying a set amount of rent. The new model Yvan was bringing in was a percentage of the sales.

While we were driving, I was telling Mel about my problems. He listened to me. Mel agreed with me it would be best if I found a new space. Then we arrived at the warehouse Mel needed to pick stuff up from. It was a great space in an industrial area., it felt fantastic. I was tingling as I walked around this showroom. The showroom was large, with a great layout. Mel got the stuff from the back that he needed and was ready to leave. I asked what this was used for as it felt so spiritual. Mel laughed and told me that this space had been used by a church. The City refused to license the church because of parking. He told me that he was going to rent it out. How much is the rent I asked? The price he gave me was affordable. I went home to ask my angels. The answer was yes. A week later, I had my new space. It has been a blessing in more ways than I can count.

Chapter Fifteen

Ghosts, and speaking from the afterlife

Let me make clear that there is a huge difference between ghosts and the deceased coming through from the other side. A ghost is in distress. They have not traveled the full length of the tunnel. The ghosts are so full of emotion, that they are unable to turn around and see what awaits them. They are still focused only on this dimension. Whereas a person coming through from the other side, has already made peace with where they are. They have seen their past lives and understand themselves perfectly. They can look across the veil and connect with mediums. They can also communicate with the angels that are around the people they love.

I have worked with thousands of people throughout the years. Through these sessions, I have come to understand some undeniable truths about our mind, soul, body connection. The reason I decided to write this book is to spread the word of hope. There is a better way to be in the world. We all can have a life with some magic in it. I have had amazing results with people from all walks of life. I am going to share some of these results with you. For privacy, I have changed names, but the events are all true.

Chapter Sixteen

Mediumship

A young woman named Gemma came to see me. I could tell she was distraught. Gemma did not share with me why she was there. As I took her hands, I saw an image of a man behind her, he identified himself as her father. He showed me that he had suffered a massive heart attack. I saw this by receiving an enormous pain in my chest. (Sometimes it would be nice if they just mind spoke). Thankfully, the pain was short-lived, as it would have been as he left his body immediately. Gemma confirmed to communicate with her dad, was the reason she had come to see me. Gemma had received the news of his death from her mother. Gemma was planning to attend his funeral on the weekend. She was flying to Ontario the next day to attend his funeral.

Her father was talking to Gemma through me. He was very verbal. I was having difficulty keeping up with him. Let me explain one of the ways I receive messages from the other side is images. I will see things in my mind that don't necessarily make sense to me. In this case, I saw a carving. It looked like a head, without features. I shared this with Gemma. I explained I had no idea what it was. I also informed her that I could see a peanut. The peanut is a symbol to me of pregnancy.

About a month later, Gemma came back to see me. She was excited to share with me what the head had represented. I will admit I was very curious. Believe it, or not, her father had made a Mr. Potato head for her son. He had been working on it before his death. It was a labor of love. Gemma also confirmed she was expecting her second child. She wanted to thank me for my gift. Gemma was so sure now that her father was watching over her, and her son. I was honoured to have been able to share with her father's words. I was also grateful that she let me know that what I had witnessed was in fact, true.

This was one f the sessions that convinced me to say what I see. If I don't understand what it means, say it anyway. Perhaps the client won't know right away either. I now know that later the message will make sense.

The little girl that I described at Maple Arbour Farm is a ghost. As well as the woman who walks around the kitchen at the farm is a ghost.

Chapter Seventeen

Past Life Regressions

I had been brought up in a Christian home. In a Christian school, I had studied to be a minister in the United Church. Therefore my belief about re-incarnation was, to say the least doubtful. I have learned though that "Spirit " is to be trusted at all times. So when George came to see me, I was open to any, and all possibilities.

George walked down the rickety stairs at New Age. George had spent six years studying to be a lawyer. At last, his goal was in sight. George displayed signs of anxiety way above a normal reaction to coming to see a psychic. I could tell that I was practically a last resort for him. I took his hands and shared my energy with him. I have a very calming effect on people. I told him about what was written in his palm. As I talked, I could feel that he started to trust me.

George was paralyzed with fear. He explained that this was not new; anxiety is a condition he suffered with. He knew that there was no way he would pass the bar. He said that he had seen my face on his GPS. He felt it was a sign that I could help him. As I listened to his angels, I was shown his past life. He had lived a life as a Nazi. George had hated what he had been forced to do. He was riddled with guilt. The more I listened and saw what his angels were telling me, the more I understood., the more his paralyzing fear made sense. He had hated being a Nazi, but if he didn't do what he was told, he would be shot. So his family had set up an underground system to hide the young people he could rescue, and he would bring to them.

I asked George about his family, as I believe we return to the same family groups for up to seven lives. Spirit informed me the whole family suffered the same anxiety problems that George did. He confirmed that they were all paralyzed with fear. His sister was hospitalized frequently as her anxiety took hold of her. I explained to George what I heard his angels say to me. Strangely it all made sense from what I understand about our souls being our memory bank.

I offered to do a past life regression and a time line clearing to remove the pain and guilt from his soul. He was grateful that I had a possible solution as he was desperate. I put George into a trance; then I led him into his life as a Nazi. It was super painful for him. As I guided him, I became aware that he had worked underground with his family to move Jews out of the country.

As I saw his past life unfurl, I could see he was a very good man. His anxiety all fell in to place. Had he or his family been caught, they too would have perished. His family had saved many people. I talked to his soul and asked his soul to allow me to remove all the pain that blocks him. As I brought him back through time and space to this life now, I gave him peace and calmness.

I installed confidence I gave him a magic spot on his ear so that any time he felt anxiety, he could pull his ear and the fear would leave him. Then I brought him back to today. I asked him to confirm what he had seen. Wen I do past life regressions, I observe what my clients are seeing. I don't tell them what to see. He told me the same story I had watched through his eyes.

By the time he left, I was sure he would go on to be a lawyer. Approximately three months later, George called and told my assistant that he had passed the bar. He told her to thank me, and that I would know who he was. I am always grateful when I get told the results. It gives me confidence as well, to keep doing what I do. As time passed, he sent me all his family members, one by one. They each received healing. Now when I have clients who have measurable anxiety, I recommend a past life regression as I did for George.

Anxiety is not the only symptom that memories in the soul are responsible for. I am relating a few more for you. This can be the most important part of healing a person's life. Remember, our souls are the windows operating system of our lives. You will learn more about this as I continue.

Janna has been a client of mine for quite a few years. After I left New Age, there was some difficulty in locating me. New Age, of course, wanted to retain my clients. However, I did a lot of promoting, so my clients started to find me. Janna found me and was desperate for help. Janna was convinced, that her daughter Reja a supermodel suffered from anorexia. Janna wanted me to help her. They had been to many doctors to no avail Janna was at her wit's end. I explained that I believed a lot of eating disorders are because of starvation in the war or being overweight in the war.

Let me explain. So anorexia is a brand new disease. This is a fear of being overweight. We know that during the war if a person was obese, it was believed they were a spy. As everyone was hungry, rationing was enough only to survive. Not thrive. Let's say you had a glandular problem. It was likely you would have been overweight. You would have been hungry and fat. (horrible thought) You would have been shunned by everyone around you. Believe me; your soul remembers that pain. Your soul remembers you telling it that you could not survive to be fat again.

On the other hand, if you are overweight, it is very often because you starved in a past life. Your soul is desperate to make sure that doesn't happen again. Therefore you eat compulsively. So I explained this to Janna. She brought her daughter in to meet me. We did some healing work with Reja. Today she is proudly walking the runway, healthy and happy.

To get the concept of this, we have to understand that "SOURCE" is also non-judgemental. That SOURCE is intelligent energy, this intelligence energy gives us what it hears from your angels. Source never says you are wrong; it just follows the law of creation. I do believe there are times when the higher angles do step in. I am talking the Christ-like or Arch Angels when they absolutely needed. I do 5'think we are going to get some interference soon. I don't want to talk politics yet would have to be blind to be unaware of the hatred that is rising to the top of our energy field. The dark evil forces are at work. Yes, evil does exist.

Chapter Eighteen

Evil

Part of my services includes doing what I call house clearings. There is real energy that can inhabit a home. Some people call it a haunted house. Like Maple Arbour Farm was a haunted house, at the time I knew it was haunted but I did not realize that the spirit was greedy for grief. I know that now.

I was called out to do a clearing on the house for a client of mine. Jane had been my client for a few years. This house was absolutely amazing. It was a smart home. It would know when you walked into a room. It would turn on lights as needed. The house had cost about 5 million dollars. It was about 6000 Sq. Ft. It was very haunted. I could feel the presence of evil when I walked in the place. I used sage and prayers throughout the house, yet I could still feel the darkness. I sat in a developed basement and prayed.

I saw a vision of a man of color. He was like a medicine man dancing around a fire. He was dancing and drumming and going wild. This didn't fit with what I knew of the house; it was only two years old. Occupied by a lovely family. I relayed what I saw to my client Jane. She was taken aback, as her husband had spent 15 years in Benin. This is the home of voodoo. Jane wanted to know if it was about her husband, was he cursed? I said no, however, there is something here in this house that attracts this evil. It turns out they had voodoo masks in the basement very close to where I was sitting. I told her to dispose of them. I then did a ritual around the house. I was praying for the inhabitant's protection. When I was finished, I took my bag and things, then as I left, I felt hands on my back and a firm push. I fell and hurt myself quite badly. I called Jane to remind her to get rid of the masks.

Not everyone listens. I am still flabbergasted when I am ignored. It does happen though, and in this case, I was totally ignored. Strangely I know that Jane believes in me, and she has referred many people to me. So that is not the problem. I think it is hard to believe that evil energy exists. Or if it exists that it can really hurt us. So anyway, Jane ignored me. I heard back from Jane when the house disintegrated around them. The windows fell out. The roof fell in, and the electric shorted out. The mold level in the house was so high it was condemned. In 24 hours, they had to get out and find a place to live.

So they found a house to rent. Their rental house is incredible as it has fantastic craftsmanship. The lady who had this built oversaw the whole process it was built with so much love. It seemed as if every single screw was blessed. Yet Jane had been sitting in the cedar-lined office working, she had an eerie feeling and walked out of the office, As she was walking out she felt the wind and a loud bang. She turned, and the Cedar lining from the ceiling had fallen down. If she had not left the office when she did, I am sure she would have been very severely injured, perhaps even dead.

I walked through this house, and I could feel and sense the care that had gone into building this property. However, I informed her that the office was a different story. I could see the medicine man in that room. I asked what she had done with the masks. Jane had given them to the movers. (I hope the movers are okay) She had not got rid of them months before. They were still in the house when it fell apart. I asked her why I could see the medicine like man. I said, you still have masks in this house. I walked into the office, sure enough, there were two masks in the office. She said well they looked harmless to me, not evil like the other ones. I, of course, removed them myself and disposed of them. I am happy to report. There have been no more incidents in their house.

Selfishness is often the root of EVIL. When a person is so greedy for pleasure that they ignore another person's feelings is when evil thrives. However never forget what the bible calls the fallen angels. That is the third of the angels, that left with Lucifer when Lucifer fought with God. These are referred to in the Quran as Jins. I have witnessed these demons take over people. I have a dear friend whose husband I love dearly. As soon as he drinks, his demon takes over. He will speak in an ancient language. He has no idea what he is saying. He will get abusive and demanding. The demon is having fun. You see the punishment that God meted out to the demons was to take away their celestial bodies. So they need to use ours. I see this quite often. I have even had a judge come to see me for an exorcism as he knew himself that he had a demon attached to him. I performed an exorcism based on the bible. A week later his wife called to thank me for giving her back her happy husband. Never discount the other dimensions. We may have difficulty seeing the other side. However they can see us quite clearly.

Chapter Nineteen

Miracles

I have a client George that walked down the rickety stairs at New Age. He was obviously nervous and desperate. He was paralyzed by fear. George had spent six years studying to be a lawyer. At last, the goal was in sight. Yet he knew that there was no way he would pass the bar. As I listened to his angels, I determined that he had lived a life as a Nazi. He hated what he had been forced to do. He was riddled with guilt. The more I listened, the more his paralyzing fear made sense. He had hated being a Nazi, but if he didn't do what he was told, he would be shot. So his family had set up an underground system to hide the young people he could rescue, and he would bring to them.

I asked George if his family suffered the same fear that he did. He confirmed that they were all paralyzed with fear. His sister was hospitalized frequently as her anxiety took hold of her. I explained to George what I heard his angels say to me. I offered to do a past life regression and a timeline clearing to remove the pain and guilt from his soul. He was grateful that I had a possible solution as he was desperate. I took him into his life as a Nazi. It was super painful for him. I told him he was a good man, he had saved many people. I talked to his soul and asked his soul to allow me to remove all the pain that blocks him. As I brought him back through time and space to this life now, I gave him peace and calmness. I installed confidence I gave him a magic spot on his ear so that any time he felt anxiety, he could pull his ear and the fear would leave him. When we were done, he was a different person. His eyes were bright, and I was sure he would go on to be a lawyer. As it happens, he actually called and told my assistant that he had passed the bar. He told her to thank me, and that I would know who he was. I am always grateful when I get told the results. It gives me confidence as well, to keep doing what I do. As time passed, he sent me all his family members, one by one; they received healing.

Emma has worked with me for at least 4 years. When Emma originally came to see me, it was about her divorce. Emma was devastated. She loved her husband very much, and was so hurt that he had left her. They had been together for 8 years and they had been trying desperately to have children. Unfortunately, even with IVF Emma had been unable to conceive. This was why her husband left as it was to hard for him to accept that they could not have a family. I worked with her to relieve the pain of his loss, and the dream of the family she wanted.

Jane was doing well in her career, and I work with her to get over nervousness. I helped her to speak well as she gives presentations. However her soul needed healing as the grief was still with her. I asked her to trust me as I did a time line healing with her. I removed her blocks and stops. Then I put a beautiful healthy baby girl in her future. Now remember I am not talking to her mind. I am talking to her soul. As the years went by I watched Emma blossom. She regained herself. It was marvellous to watch as she blossomed.

On November 10th 2018, Emma walked in to the studio. I turned and said "Congratulations, Your pregnant." Well let me tell you, she was mad. Emma said "Judy of all the people I trust its you. So you know I only have one egg left and I am 42 years old. I cannot have a baby. The doctors told me its like a trillion to one chance, that I would ever conceive. So for you to say that is painful." I apologized, and explained, its not me that is saying it. Your angels told me you are pregnant.

I didn't hear from Emma again until the January of 2019. So two months later. Emma was struggling with a person at work, and was asking for advice. I looked at her and said "are you pregnant?" She said "yes I left you a message". I had not got the message but was over the moon for her. In July she gave birth to a beautiful baby girl. Her new partner and Emma are delighted. So are the grandparents on both sides. The power of communicating correctly with a persons soul creates miracles.

Mary is a young 32 year old Irish woman, she was a brand new client to me. When I was doing he reading I looked at her palm and her life line ended at 32. I don't ever tell a person if I see something like that but I dig deep. I told her that I saw and illness. I explained that I offer a time line clearing that removes things in the soul that effect a persons life negatively. I did her whole reading. She was convinced I was the real deal, as she put it. Mary asked more about the process. I explained that I usually had people do a 30 day program prior to doing the time line process. I told her I would make and exception as I could feel that this was imminent.

Mary came back the next day and I proceeded with the time line. I spent extra time installing a bright happy healthy future for her. I was sure it had helped as when she left my office her eyes were bright and shiny. All of a sudden I was inundated with young Irish clients. One after the other they came all referred by Mary. I didn't question it particularly as that does happen. However 2 months later Mary herself returned. I took her hands to feel her energy. She was bursting with excitement. I could feel the zing all through me. I looked at her palms and low and behold her life line was now right around her wrist. This indicates a long life.

Mary then shared with me that she had a brain tumour when she first came to see me. The surgery was scheduled for three weeks down the road. That was why she could not wait the four weeks that I had recommended. Mary had come in to share with me the results of our session. She shared that when they took her in to prep her for surgery they did a mapping of her head to locate exactly where the tumour was. She had had the mapping before, however they needed to do this as they prepared her for surgery. This surgery was very risky, Mary could be paralyzed or lose her speech. Or other handicaps even death. When they looked at the mapping her tumour was gone. Thats right not a trace was left. The doctors were shocked and delighted for her. Mary told them what I had done with her. They were skeptical, but could not argue with the results.

Chapter Twenty

Our Souls

The soul is programmed by events that have occurred either in this life or past lives.
For example, let's say you are married, and your husband cheated on you. You are so emotional about this. Every time he leaves the house you worry, Is he going to be with someone else.? You are in constant fear that he is going to leave you. For some unexplained reason, you want him to stay no matter the cost. Your soul is content to let this continue because you are so emotional, Your soul knows you are alive, and it is succeeding in its first job, and its second job. You, of course, are very unhappy and trying to find a way out. So next step your husband leaves you he says he cannot take the distrust etc. anymore. Now you

go through turmoil and upset, your soul is still ok because your emotions are still high.

Then low and behold you, heal and feel okay about yourself. Things turn out okay, maybe you go to school and land a good job and therefore you are feeling great. Your soul is happy. Then you get bored, your emotions are low. Your soul is not sure what's going on so your soul springs into action. Your soul brings you another man your feelings are high again. Your soul is working well. Then he cheats, now your emotions are intense your soul is doing its job. Too well, some might say! However, this is the way it works. How many people do you know that are in a relationship with the same person in a different body? I know it sounds hopeless, but there are ways to make this all work for you, not against you.

I was with a client Tammy, she had come to me in December of 2016. She was extremely anxious about her father's health. I told her that I felt he had stomach cancer. She persisted and asked me if he was going to survive. I resisted answering her, but she remained insistent on its importance it was for her to know. I explained that I did not like to predict death as one of the rules my mother had told me was about planting seeds.

However, I did see him passing away in the April. My angels, insisted I tell her. So I had told her what I heard before, she left. Now in April 2017, she came back to see me, and as I touched her hand, I observed her father on the other side. He was hiding behind a tree. I was surprised by this. I questioned Tammy as to why her father would be hiding behind a tree. Tammy laughed and told me he was a Jehovah's Witness and didn't believe in psychics. He would be hiding even in the afterlife we want to be right. That is when I realized that the souls need to make us, right is eternal. So when people talk about limiting beliefs. This is what is essential for us to understand. If we can reprogram our souls to believe things that serve us, our lives can be magical. This is what I intend to teach you as we go further into my program.

We have so much wrapped up in the things that our parents planted in our memory banks that we get lost in our quest for a better life. The only way I know to set us free is to love them anyway. I always recall my mother taking me to the Accident and Orthopaedic Hospital with her. This is where she worked in Sunderland. A lot of the patients did not get many visitors, so we would go in on a Sunday and be the visitors. One particular Sunday, while I was visiting the patients, I saw a little girl crying her eyes out for her mummy. I saw that she was very severely burnt. I was concerned.

I asked my mum why the little girl's mum wasn't with her. Mum spoke very low and explained that the mother was in jail because the mother had thrown boiling water over her daughter. That is why the little girl was so severely burnt. I was astonished, then why is she asking for her mum? My mum explained that we have a need to love our parents, and to believe that they love us. I have so much evidence that mum was, and is right. The need to love our parents can be the number one cause of limiting beliefs. Unfortunately, it can be the hardest to overcome, as well. Your parents may have an addiction problem. When this is the case, there is a good chance that you will either have addictions or be an addiction counsellor.

If one of your parents went to jail, there is a chance you will go to jail. Or be a policeman or lawyer. The influence of our parents on our soul is this profound. If your parents were single parents, There is a big chance you would follow in those footsteps. It seems that the more we disapprove, of our parents, the more control this rule leads our lives. A study showed that 75% of welfare families continue on to the next generation. 80% of people that come from a broken home go on to live in a fractured home themselves. Our soul puts us in these situations so that we get to see why our parents were the way they were. By following in their footsteps, we understand their hardships. When we know their reasons, we forgive and accept them. This is huge in our soul as it is one of the first four primary directives of the soul.

Where your Focus Goes, Energy Flows, Results Show!

What does all this Mean?

So let's take a look at our Sacred Ladder.

Your soul has this sacred ladder that moves up to source (God)

It starts with your soul, which is located at the solar plexus region of your body. When we die, this soul leaves us and continues on its journey. See picture (Sacred Ladder).

The next rung on the ladder is our body. This is why our soul affects our health, which I can show again and again. I would refer you to "Love Laughter and Medicine" by Dr. Bernie Segal. Your soul is also the 21 grams that leave us when we die.

The next level is your emotional body. I think of this as the connecting cord to our angels and source. I know that each of us has the emotional capacity to move mountains. We wake up our spiritual body with the power of our feelings. Emotions and feelings are essential to the soul. People send to their souls the negative emotions or worries that they dwell on. Our souls get excited and continue to give us more of those events that caused the emotion in the first place. This is how the soul does its job. The good news is If we send our soul emotions that are our desires, our soul gives us our desired outcome. Your feelings are the telephone cord to your angels. Ring them with consciousness. The results improve.

The final level before source (God) is our angel body.

This is the body of Angels that interpret everything for source. This is the body that responds to us and is the communication field between us and God (source) at all times. Our angels are assigned to us at birth. They are with us through all our lives. Sometimes they need a shove or kick up the butt. This is why when someone who loves you dies, your life can be rocked. Your loved one goes and straightens out your angels. It is like they knock on the angel's door and explain you don't want the bad stuff to repeat.

I had a client that went through my program, and she indeed did everything to get a better result. Yet she was still single unhappy and unable to connect well with others. So she asked me to fire her angels. Well, when I stopped laughing, I understood that she felt her angels were not listening to her. They were so used to delivering the same old pain, that they were not changing with her. I put a lot of thought into how to handle this and decided that I needed to fire her angels.

So on the full blood moon, I took myself and my client Michelle and two other people To my spiritual space and lit a fire. Then I performed a powerful ritual. This ritual was asking to bring in new angels as we thanked the old ones for keeping her safe. Then we did a dance and ceremony to invite in new angels that would bring her love light and happiness. These angels were to listen to her and deliver her wants. Now I do not know if her beliefs changed with the ritual, or if the angels changed. However, I can report that she is now happily married and doing great in her life.

Talking to your angels is a great place to start. The more excited you are, the more they pay attention. This is why emotions are so important. They do not judge, they deliver. What they hear is what you get. Where you focus goes, energy flows, and results show.

Get excited about your life!
Let's Make a Change!
Let's Create a Life worth Living.
Ready, Set, Go!

Soul Lessons Learned.

I have worked with thousands of people throughout the years. I have come to understand some undeniable truths about our mind, soul, body connection. The reason I decided to write this book is to spread the word of hope. There is a better way to be in the world. We all can have a life with some magic in it. I have had amazing results with people from all walks of life. I am going to share some of these results with you. For privacy, the names of my clients have been changed, but the events are all true.

What is Soul? Let's do the exploration of "who are you."

Our Soul is Eternal.

I spend many hours communicating daily with people that have passed. These deceased people are sending messages for their loved ones that come to inquire about them. I used to think that perhaps I was mind reading and was delivering to people what they were thinking about. Yet so many times, the inquirer had no knowledge of the information I receive from the departed.

What does it mean that the soul is eternal?

It means that we never cease to be. We are not in the human body. In my experience, we move into different states of being. We do, however, always exist. It fascinates me that when we pass, we can see all of our past lives. I experience some people saying oh that's why I was afraid of water etc. Is reincarnation real? This is what I have come to believe. Yet not everyone wants to return here and live another human existence.

The Soul is our memory bank.

Every life that we have lived and every experience we have had. Every emotion we have felt is stored in our soul. We have proved many times over that people are affected by past life experiences. Like the little boy in India who led his new parents to his murderer and his old parents. These stories are repeated frequently and can not be disputed. In my experience, even very ordinary lives are affected by past life memories.

Jobs of the Soul!
SURVIVAL!

The first job of the soul in the human form is to make sure we survive.

What does this mean? It means all of our experiences are being monitored by our soul. The soul, in effect, acts as the Windows operating system. It is always running in the background, storing information. Just like in the Windows Operating System, we have cookies that mean we get information quickly based on our past searches. A cookie has more power as you give emotion to the event. Our souls also act's on our past experiences. For example, infertility seems to be connected to this survival program.

Let us say in a past life you lost a child, the pain of this loss is stored in your soul (the memory bank). When this happened, you told your soul that you would never survive this pain again. So in this life, even though you have every desire to have children, you just cannot. I have encountered this many times in my practice. The soul believes that you cannot risk having a child because you would not survive the loss. To remove this block, I take the person back and reprogram the soul. Then they can conceive a child without fear. This has worked many times to the joy of the clients.

The Next job of the Soul is Emotions.

I get that this sounds strange after the survival bit, but it is true. Your soul monitors you for emotions. Your soul monitors your feelings as a barometer of how well it is doing its job. The more you feel, the more your soul knows you are alive. However, do not forget what I told you about being non-judgemental! So, in other words, the soul does not monitor for good feelings or bad feelings, as long as you are feeling. This can lead to a repeat of awful feelings. Remember the cookies I told you about.

The soul is non-judgmental.

The knowledge in our soul, the memories we have stored the experiences we have had are there. They are not good or bad; they are just there. This is the most valuable component part of what I have come to understand. As you read and understand the sessions, I am sharing with you. It must become evident that the soul doesn't disseminate for you. If it did, it would know that you need to eat and would make sure you do. It would give you what you desire, not what you don't want. All of us can attest to the fact terrible things happen. As it is true that the soul is sending messages always to our spirit body (I like to call them our angels), then our angels translate these messages into the language of the intelligent energy people call God. This is the Law of the universe. Some people call it the Law of Attraction. It isn't the Law of attraction that is a misnomer; it is the Law of creation. This is automatic and ongoing at all times. What we put in our soul we send to our angels. The tool that controls what the angels hear is emotion. The more feeling, the stronger the message is. The faster it moves through the layers and reaches the source. I have a saying. It is one of my daily "Judyism's ." It goes like this " You can always tell a person's beliefs by the results." In other words, your life is a reflection of your soul.

The next job of the Soul is to make you right.

Yes! That is correct. The soul makes you right all the time. Understand this please, we are creating our life. This is occurring all the time. You are not just creating when you think about it. You are creating all the time. Your soul will always make you correct. When you believe that, you will find it easy to pass tests. Then on tests, you will consistently perform well. If you see yourself as attractive, other people will let you know you are beautiful. This even works in the afterlife. It was one of my aha moments.

The next job of the soul is to accept your parents and Love God.

Acceptance is LOVE. We take everything we learn as a child into our Soul.

Psychiatrists call it our subconscious mind, but I know this subconscious to be our soul. My sincere hope is you will understand this level of need within each person. All people are born, needing knowledge of God. To have a relationship with God. This need for acceptance, connection, or belonging is prevalent throughout the centuries in all cultures, religions, and communities. In every form, mankind has had knowledge that there is something more than a man. It is in the cave mans pictures and all written history. Man has been on a quest to know and understand God. Yet it is the one thing people fight about more than anything else.. Yet it is evident through each and every scripture. Through the teaching of any of the masters from Jesus Christ to the Buddha, there is one commonality; God wants us to love one another. Not by color or creed, but because love heals everything. I believe that as hate rises, the understanding and acceptance of LOVE will make way for the dissipation of hatred. God is intelligent energy. God is everywhere in all things. Once we understand the power of creation, we will find love.

We think when we are children that our parents are omnipotent. Therefore when we reach a certain age, we realize they are not right about everything, and in a lot of cases, we feel misled and angry that we were taught untruths. It is when we understand that our parents are human and make mistakes, we should accept them as they are. Then freedom from our parent's stuff is realized.

Chapter Twenty-One

Soul Lessons Learned

After spending all these years helping people transform their lives I believe that our souls are programmed to get us attention. This starts in the crib. After we cry mummy comes. When we are hurt mummy comes. If we are suffering people pay attention. If there is drama in our lives we get attention. Misery loves company and so on.

This way of being is our genetic memory from our past lives, and our childhoods. It is acceptable as nearly everyone does it. At the end of the day it is a habit that is programmed in our soul. We focus on the pain in our lives and we talk about it to other people. If someone starts to talk about how great their life is. Other people tend to put them down.

As we all should know by now habits can be broken. This is hard work and takes time but it is worth it. My next book will be my 30 day program to run the anti-virus software for your soul. I truly hope this book has opened your heart to a better understanding and love of self and others.

In the words of the great St. Francis of Assisi.

Remember that when you leave this earth, you can take with you nothing that you have received - only what you have given: a full heart, enriched by honest service, love, sacrifice and courage.

Made in the USA
Middletown, DE
09 September 2019